MW00679953

40-DAY DEVOTIONAL FOR PARENTS

A Parenting Doctor's Call to Fill Your Children's Lamp with Oil through Prayer and Action

Daniel J. van Ingen, Psy .D.

This book and the book *You Are Your Child's Best Psychologist: 7 Keys to Excellence in Parenting* are available at special quantity discounts for bulk purchase for sales promotions, premiums, fund-raising, and educational needs. For details, call us at 612-501-5358, email us at danieljvaningen@gmail.com or visit our website at: www.parentingdoctors.com

40-Day Devotional For Parents: A Parenting Doctor's Call To Fill Your Children's Lamp with Oil through Prayer and Action by Daniel J. van Ingen
Published by Parent Doctor Publishing
Sarasota, Florida, USA

This book or parts thereof may not be reproduced in any form, stored in a retrieval system, or transmitted in any form by any means—electronic, mechanical, photocopy, recording, or otherwise—without prior written permission of the publisher, except as provided by United States of America copyright law.

Unless otherwise noted, all Scripture quotations are taken from the New King James Version®. Copyright © 1982 by Thomas Nelson. Used by permission. All rights reserved.

Scripture quotations marked NIV are taken from the Holy Bible, New International Version® , NIV®. Copyright © 1973, 1978, 1984, 2011 by Biblica, Inc.® Used by permission of Zondervan. All rights reserved worldwide. www.zondervan.com. The "NIV" and "New International Version" are trademarks registered in the United States Patent and Trademark Office by Biblica, Inc.®

Scripture quotations marked TPT are from The Passion Translation®. Copyright © 2017, 2018 by Passion & Fire Ministries, Inc. Used by permission. All rights reserved. ThePassionTranslation.com.

Copyright © 2020 by Daniel J. van Ingen
All rights reserved

Visit the author's websites at www.danvaningen.com,
www.parentingdoctors.com

Library of Congress Cataloging-in-Publication Data:
An application to register this book for cataloging has been submitted
to the Library of Congress.
International Standard Book Number: 978-1-7357048-0-7

While the author has made every effort to provide accurate internet
addresses at the time of publication, neither the publisher nor the
author assumes any responsibility for errors or for changes that occur
after publication.

Parenting Doctors

Endorsements

"Dr. van Ingen has produced a masterful tool for parents. As parents, we know that our most important assignment in life is the development of our children's faith and self-image. However, we also feel inadequate and afraid, thus we are prone to avoid developing our children in hopes that they will pick up our values via osmosis. Dr. van Ingen's devotional will help you in a very practical and inspirational manner. I would highly recommend this devotional for every parent that desires to help their children discover and develop their faith and self-identity!"

Pastor Richard Crisco
Senior Pastor
Rochester Christian Church
Founder & President of Empowering Kingdom Leaders

"Raising our children with the guidance of the Lord is such a crucial topic, in my opinion. As a parent and grandparent (GiGi) myself, I have always felt that parenting is one of the most important callings you could ever receive from the Lord. Henceforth, providing tools that will help us learn and grow as parents is exactly what Daniel van Ingen has accomplished in this incredible 40-Day Devotional for Parents. Throughout this devotional, you will feel the gentle aid from one parent to another as you gain insight and advice from not only Daniel's understanding but also from the beautiful counsel in the Word of God. As you read Daniel's words, I hope you will find comfort in knowing that none of us have all of the answers in regards to raising our children, but through seeking instruction and assistance, we can grow to become everything that God has intended us to be for our precious children."

Jeri Hill
Co-founder and President
Together in the Harvest

"Excellent! Full of poignant truth and wisdom. Dan is able to zero in on important and practical ideas without 'fluff' and clichés."

Jedd Hafer
Founder, Mission Peace

"Great topics! Applicable, practical, relevant, biblical, doable and spot on. This will help a lot of parents who have done it wrong, who don't know what to do, do it like they were raised, or never knew where to start. This will encourage, equip, empower, and enable people to spend meaningful time with their kids and set healthy boundaries as parents and not from a perspective of their kids "friend." I loved it."

Chris Hall
Restoring The Foundations
Healing House Network

Dr. Daniel van Ingen's work is one of the most practical yet thought-provoking texts on both spiritual development and discipleship I have seen in a while. Dr. van Ingen addresses both personal spiritual formation and evidenced-based practice for an excellent work on wholeness. Wherever one is in their spiritual journey, they can begin with this text making advancements for themselves and their children. I fully recommend this text for pastors, teachers and lay-persons because individual growth can positively impact the lives of those around you for now and eternity.

Dr. Justin Kidd
Senior Pastor
Antioch Baptist Church

This book covers a wide range of extremely important issues which all families need to address. The author reveals his knowledge of our current cultural climate and how those who want to follow Christ and live a life worth living must not be influenced by what everyone else is doing. Every family can benefit by focusing on the 40 topics highlighted in this short book. Apply the lessons taught in this book and change your family's destiny.

Hugh Houston
Author of JESUS IS BETTER THAN PORN: How I Confessed my Addiction to My Wife and Found a New Life

"40-Day Devotional for Parents: A Parenting Doctor's Call to Fill Your Children's Lamp with Oil through Prayer and Action" is an excellent read dedicated to incorporating prayer in rearing our children. As a dedicated follower of Jesus Christ and father of two, I appreciate Dr. van Ingen's devotional book given today's climate with child-raising. In his book, Dr. van Ingen provides a devotional for 40 key areas affecting children today. Each daily reading is accompanied with supporting biblical scriptures and focus questions to further drive home the point. The devotional can be used for personal reading or in a classroom setting. I believe this book does an excellent job of emphasizing a necessary component for all elements of parenting.....PRAYER. Great read! Job well done Dr. van Ingen!"

Ndidi Madu, D.O.
Family Practitioner

"Dr. van Ingen's devotional offers the much-needed wisdom of the Gospel with psychological insights that will greatly help families facing the challenges of parenting in the modern world."

Fr. Eric Scanlan, STL
Administrator of Incarnation Catholic Church

40 Day Devotional

CONTENTS

Foreword

By Jeri Hill, Co-Founder & President of Together in the Harvest

Story of Ryan Hill & Encouragement for Other Parents

If you are opening this devotional already feeling weighed down and burdened by guilt and shame as a parent, I want you to know that you are not alone. Sometimes we have this image in our head that people who write parenting books or even endorse these kinds of books are "perfect" parents. That couldn't be further from the truth. In fact, most of us are trying to learn how to parent just like everyone else.

You see, the Lord blessed my husband and me with three beautiful children. Although He blessed us with an incredible marriage, family, ministry and we were able to share the Gospel around the world together, we still had struggles at home in regard to raising our children. After my incredible husband, Steve Hill's passing, my only son Ryan suddenly passed away from an accidental overdose just seven months later. Now, I mentor women all over

1

the world and train them to become Godly wives, mothers, teachers, evangelists, and the list goes on and on. How could I continue to mentor people when I myself feel like my entire world has crashed down around me?

Through the past several years, I have dealt with heavy guilt, shame and grief. I could've given up in the darkest times of my despair (and trust me, I want to), yet I always felt the gentle nudging of the Holy Spirit to simply "keep going." To be completely honest though, there were definitely days when I just wanted to hide away in a metaphorical cave and escape from everyone. You may be reading this and may feel the exact same way. Mom, Dad, you're not alone. You'd be surprised to know of how many parents/grandparents are out there who are going through the same feelings you are experiencing.

At the end of the day, we cannot control all of the choices our children make, especially when they become adults. The best thing we can do is pray for them as we release our children into God's hands and trust Him with their lives. No matter what has happened, if I could encourage you with anything, I would tell you to "keep going." Allow the gentle nudging of the Holy Spirit to guide you step by step. You may feel like your sails are down right now, but trust me when I say this, you don't have to feel like this forever. The Lord has such a merciful way of slowly putting wind back in your sails. As you spend time in God's presence, read His Word, and follow along in Daniel J. van Ingen's 40-Day Devotional for Parents, I pray you will begin to feel encouragement from the Lord. I pray you experience His loving arms begin to pick you back up again and set you on your feet. Before you know it, He will use your testimony to help others get back on their feet again as well, just as He has done for me. I don't know the pain you have experienced, but I know one thing is for sure, it is never too late to be used by God!

Introduction

⁓ ❧ ⁓

I wrote a book titled "You Are Your Child's Best Psychologist: 7 Keys to Excellence in Parenting." This book has been endorsed by pediatricians, psychologists, professors, parents, grandparents, Christians, atheists, business people, social workers, former addicts, and some of the best pastors I know. I've received endorsements from a 2-time pediatrician of the year Ted Meyer, M.D., in Sarasota County and a college basketball national coach of the year and national champion in John Tauer, Ph.D., who authored a key book on youth sports. In response to the positive response we received, a colleague of mine encouraged me to write a devotional that captured the 40 most pressing areas of prayer for parents. I thought, "Wow, this will be exciting!" But, how do you capture the 40 areas of prayer? I didn't want to just take the 40 best ideas and now apply prayer. This work had to come from a deep place, a location that can only be found through prayer and devotion to the Lord of all. Every one of us needs to find that quiet inner place and seek the Lord. After being baptized by John the Baptist, **Jesus** fasted for **40 days** and nights in the Judaean Desert. Each day centers on an important area of prayer for our children over the next 40 days. This will be a great opportunity to both seek the Lord by pursuing the Father's heart and pursue prayer in 40 key areas for your children.

One of the things I say about my book "*You Are Your Child's Best Psychologist: 7 Keys to Excellence in Parenting*" is that it has the best information on parenting. Actually, applying it is the hard part. I struggle as much as the next mom or dad trying to apply the best wisdom and knowledge that we know about parenting. The things that matter most are those things that come from a place of depth. And the best way to apply what we know is with love deeply embedded in prayer. Parents have been very favorable and positive towards *You Are Your Child's Best Psychologist: 7 Keys to Excellence in Parenting*, primarily for its practical common sense and solution-focused wisdom. This devotional address what was missing in the book—the need for prayer in the 40 most pressing areas in child-raising.

When I was 22 years old, I had an incredible transformation when I encountered the Lord Jesus Christ on November 8th, 1997. On a Saturday night in Bloomington, Minnesota, I experienced a profound conversion at a prayer meeting facilitated by the People of Praise Christian Community, who were deeply impacted by the Brownsville Revival. This was an ecumenical Christian community comprised primarily of Catholics who were deeply affected by Assemblies of God and

Pentecostals! Amazing! On that night, I encountered the person of Jesus in an incredible way. His love and intimacy overwhelmed my consciousness and repaired my heart.

We want to pray that every child, pre-teen, and teenager will experience a profound encounter with the Lord. He shows up and can rupture a child's consciousness. Encounters with God facilitate burning hearts and bring incredible changes, and they can happen anywhere – alone, at church, at school -- anywhere. I pray that Jesus can reveal himself to your children. It's happening around the world. I pray that it can happen in your home now.

When I was 43 years old, I received an integrated biblical ministry by Restoring The Foundations (RTF) and experienced profound healing in a number of deep areas in my life. Despite serving people as a clinical psychologist for 15+ years, I had allowed a number of personal problem areas develop, including anger, frustration, bitterness, blaming, condemnation, criticalness, judging, unforgiveness, and discouragement. I had allowed fears to infiltrate my life despite doing research, speaking across the country, and having published a book on the best methods for treating fear and anxiety. Just because something is in the head doesn't mean this is applied to the heart. People around me wouldn't even know these things were happening in my life. Only those closest knew of my struggles. I had allowed a shame-fear-control stronghold to negatively affect my close relationships. The ministry I received was bathed in prayer. Regardless of the church, type of ministry, events or crusades, the most significant personal transformations that occur are bathed in prayer. The next 40 days is an opportunity to bathe yourself as a parent and cover key areas in your children's lives with prayer.

Joyfully Praying Out of Pain, Grief, & Loss

I also want to share about the deeper levels of pain that served as a building block for this devotional. As we age and transition from year to year and decade to decade, it becomes clear that we acquire a lot of emotional (and physical) pain. The Lord heals and restores, but some pains endure over time.

In my work as a clinical psychologist, I have dealt with extraordinary pain. My emotional pain started several years ago when a client I had worked with committed suicide. I actually treated him for the traumatic memory of his father committing suicide. His father hung himself on a tree in a forest. As part of treatment, we did trauma therapy of that traumatic memory episode. Over a series of sessions, the trauma therapy helped my client experience healing from the trauma. Symptoms like flashbacks and nightmares had gone down as a result of the therapy. He reported not having anxiety, distressing memories, physiological distress, and triggered memories of finding his father after he took his own life. He reported healing from the traumatic memory. Unfortunately, I learned one year later that this client hit a major wall in his life and ended up taking his own life in the same way his father did. He actually hung himself on the same tree in the same spot of the forest where his dad hung himself. I was stunned and deeply saddened by this experience. The truth is, I didn't share this story for years because of shame and embarrassment. Some of the following thoughts would act as oppressors in my consciousness. "This is what I do." "How would this look to others?" "What would it say about my work if the primary thing that I do is keep people alive?" Genuine oppressing thoughts included, "How did I let him down?" "What part of him was not healed that I actually thought was healed?" It took me a long time to realize that these kinds of thought patterns came from a place of shame in my own life. I was operating out of a place of insecurity and fear rather than a place of Godly identity and love. From this place of insecurity, these doubts and oppressing thoughts included self-blame. I had blamed myself for his passing. I had to allow the Lord to free me from this guilt and shame. I had to release the emotional burden I took on for many years at the foot of the cross. The truth is, I held on to the emotional burden far too long. Reflecting on this has made me realize that we hold on to things in our children's lives more than we release to the Lord. As you go through this devotional, you may find that there are emotional burdens that you have taken on in your parenting, and the Lord wants to release these burdens in your life.

To compound this challenge, my work with difficult and emotional trauma continued. I went on to hear trauma stories in extreme numbers. Stories of injured, molested, raped, and killed children repeatedly broke my heart. Over the years, I went on to hear the worst stories imaginable, including extreme sexual abuse and grotesque, violent acts. I took the time to estimate the frequency of trauma stories that I have heard in extensive detail. There were some weeks when I heard more than five horrifying stories in one week. I've actually counted hearing over 1,000 detailed trauma stories in interviews, evaluations and treatment. I've heard the stories of over 75 military sexual traumas as part of compensation & pension examinations through the VA Medical Center. Over time, the detailed descriptions of these traumatic events had a significant emotional toll on my life.

I've detailed accounts of more than 500 combat traumas, events in people's lives that a veteran experienced that involved actual death or serious injury (i.e., improvised explosive device, incoming artillery, rocket or mortar fire, grenade, sniper fire, etc.). People are haunted for life when they have to collect body parts after a plane propeller killed a person. The worst stories are those about children: children burned in fires, sex slavery, child abduction, rapes, explosive devices taped to their chests, and kidnapping. A mother was forced to watch her daughter be raped. Many horrifying stories were heard from Ukrainian refugees from the War in Donbass who settled in the St. Petersburg – Tampa area after coming to the U.S. Additionally, significant trauma was carried in the Somalian refugees following the Ethiopian Invasion of Somalia.

I have cried with parents who just lost their children in fires and car accidents. There are no easy answers for a crying mom whose child was sexually molested by an uncle. There is nothing worse in life than losing your own child, especially by a bullet right in front of you! No level of pain and suffering is equivalent to losing your child to leukemia or a brain tumor.

Over the years, I have learned some very hard lessons as I absorbed all of these stories but didn't properly dispose of them emotionally. Every day I returned to the lion's den of deep and hidden vulnerability. Each day I returned to those windows of vulnerability to hear the worst of human suffering. I constantly told myself, "I'm trained; I can handle it." The idea of burnout was always for someone else. I pridefully believed that I was a psychological superman, and I told myself scriptures like Phillipians 4:13 and applied the words that I would "do greater things" to my actual redemptive work in psychological services. The truth is—I wasn't a psychological superman. Every day I gradually stuffed the deeply painful stories and compartmentalized the horror of detailed accounts of trucks running over children and other horrific traumas. To be frank, I gradually stuffed these stories down over and over. It took me a long time to realize that I developed a 3-step sequence to hearing evil: (1) stuff down, (2) overanalyze, (3) and compartmentalize.

A few years ago, I experienced a physical threat, and my reaction revealed my psychological and spiritual burnout. I was attacked by a war veteran who suffered from psychological trauma and psychosis. He had picked up my office table and threw it on my back while he had a psychotic episode. He stood over me, screaming illogical threatening statements. My colleague, a family practice physician, heard me yelling for help, and came into my office to help talk him down. I was relieved to escape without injury. Afterwards, I chalked it up as another "incident on the job." I also had a deeply painful reaction that I was silent about for many years. Something that I never shared with anyone, not even those closest to me, was the way I handled myself when I was attacked by this aggressor who struggled with mental illness in addition to post-traumatic stress disorder. Rather than using my space, physically shifting myself using physical intervention and maneuvering techniques to safely getaway as I had been trained in the past, I actually huddled against the wall on my knees. I was immensely frightened with my arms over my head, shaking and pleading for help from the MD down the hall. The man was standing over me, screaming and threatening my life. When my colleague came in and talked the man down, I ran out of the office and toward the back of the building. My body shook for at least a ½ hour. When the police arrived, I still recall my hand shaking as I wrote up the baker act forms for the police to escort him to the hospital.

When I went on to share this story, I never mentioned my intense fear, my huddled position, and my shaking even to those closest to me. I was intensely embarrassed and refrained from sharing this part of the story to my own family. After all, I was "psychological superman." Yes, I was a victim of my own impression management and an unwillingness to be vulnerable due to pride. I also wanted to immediately suppress my feelings. For a long time, I remained confounded and perplexed as to why I didn't use trained maneuvers to get myself safe. Upon reflection, I can only conclude that fear, shock, and burnout are the culprits. Once again, I stuffed this event down. I didn't take time to feel. I didn't take time to heal. As usual, my stuffed feelings came out in other unhealthy ways.

There is a lot to learn from my failure of not taking care of and not loving myself. The "stuff down" might be a classic old school technique, but it doesn't work for a clinical psychologist. It certainly doesn't work for any pastor or parent dealing with the trials and tribulations of life. I took on all of these burdens but failed to live a balanced life. My unbalanced life involved going several years without exercising, taking on sugar addiction, engaging in unhealthy smartphone dependence, and isolating without solid male friendships. Think about this—I went years without exercise. We know exercise is critical for heart health as well as stress management. I ate ice cream or pie every night for 25 years. To give you an idea of my sugar addiction, I was in China having just walked on the Great Wall of China, and I was still craving ice cream that night. Somehow, this amazing adventure did not produce enough dopamine, and I still had cravings. This went on for many years.

This unbalanced life of exercise avoidance, sugar dependence, screen sickness, and isolation prevented freedom from reigning in my life. I experienced an L5-S1 herniated disc in my back from all of the sitting without exercise and with sugar excess. Consequently, I experienced physical numbing to match my emotional numbing. It is important for a pastor, psychologist, or counselor (or anyone) to engage with the outer world, pray deeply, intercede, and immerse himself or herself with a healthy approach to these four areas: regular exercise, healthy nutrition, healthy use of digital media and healthy relationships. I chose the "overwhelmed with life" trap resulting in zero exercise, addiction to sugar, social isolation camouflaged as self-sufficiency, and compulsive behaviors from getting hooked on my screens.

I want to share some factors and their definitions that contributed to my no exercise, sugar excess, screen sickness, and relationship isolation. First, compassion fatigue is a state of exhaustion and dysfunction – biologically, psychologically and socially – as a result of prolonged exposure to compassion stress. This is an issue that many parents struggle with and need to be prepared to address in their life. And there are degrees to this. Obviously, most soccer moms don't appear to have dysfunction on the outside. Many parents appear to have it all together as do many ER doctors. Yet, we are all struggling as life is hard. Compassion fatigue is real. Second, burnout is a generalized state of physical, emotional, and mental exhaustion that psychologists, counselors or other professionals like EMTs experience by long-term involvement in emotionally demanding situations. Parents in difficult work environments need to have a prevention plan to keep a work and personal life balance. Two additional terms sort of flow together. Secondary trauma is the manifestation of posttraumatic symptoms in clinicians when exposed to clients' stories of traumatic experiences. Finally, vicarious traumatization is a change in the clinician's inner experience and sense of self as a result of empathic engagement with the traumatic material of clients. Some of the ways this showed up in my life is that I became emotionally numb and overly analytical at times. I became overly sensitive, overly critical, defensive, and would over-explain myself. I simply believed that I could approach this work like "psychological superman" without gradually losing my gentleness and tenderness in my personal life. The bottom line is that my professional experience overwhelmed my personal inner experience. I developed a hardened and calloused heart. There were emotional consequences to my unhealthy 3-step process of stuffing, overanalyzing, and compartmentalizing. My burnout led to relational consequences, including personal stonewalling, lacking empathy, and being overly sensitive to perceiving hurt. This led me to be preemptive at times during discussions and arguments. While some of the aforementioned details in my stories are extreme—I have learned that reduced empathy is not that different from other parents who have demanding work lives. I also knew that in my field, empathy was critical, so fractured empathy compounded my personal problems. I learned the hard way that abandoning and neglecting a life of emotional health – limited physical activity, feeding the carb and sugar cravings, submitting to phone addiction, and active isolation is a recipe for emotional disaster.

When I received ministry in May 2019, I was deeply blessed through Restoring The Foundations (RTF). My foundation was restored in significant ways. For three days, I engaged in an incredible time of prayer with two ministers Chris and Dot Hall, in Naples, Florida. The prayer was spaced out over several sessions and emphasized key areas in my life that brought freedom and release of control. Some highlights of the prayer sessions included healing from word curses, negative words, the hardness of heart, compartmentalizing, emotional pain, criticalness, emotional numbness, and reduced empathy. Godly beliefs were reinforced to counter my bitterness and resentments, canceling ungodly soul ties, which included ties to things such as phones and screens, healing from trauma wounds, healing from compassion fatigue, and experiencing breakthroughs from shame-fear-control strongholds in my life. What is the shame-fear-control stronghold? As you can imagine, my former patient committing suicide was an example of a shaming event. My response to being attacked by my patient was a shaming event. I had other areas of shame, including compulsive behaviors, addictive behaviors, and poor coping strategies. We use control out of fear that others will find out about some things in us that we don't like or things we have done. We use control to avoid pain. When we lose control, everything goes away, and the healing Spirit of God has his way. The love of God penetrates deep places. Through this process with RTF, the weights that I carried on my shoulders were taken off. My foundation was tremendously restored.

While it's a process, my numbness has transitioned back to empathy. My hardness has transitioned back to tenderness. Life has a way of hardening us. The hard things of life have a way of building up callouses around our hearts. Hearing stories of evil over and over built callouses. My heart hardened and as much as I want to point to a completely transformative moment, I have learned that my journey is a process of softening again.

In addition to the freedom in God that I have experienced once again, I have taken significant steps of action. These action steps allow me to engage in my mission as a psychologist without unhealthy behaviors and addiction. The person of Jesus and these action steps are my maintenance plan that helps prevent me from experiencing compassion fatigue, burnout, secondary trauma, and vicarious traumatization.

First of all, I have now set a goal to exercise regularly. I had to look at myself and acknowledge that I became fat and then gradually (and joyfully) got used to being reminded of this fact by my children. I was overweight, lethargic, relying on sugar, and completely susceptible to future health problems. I was looking at my future of heart disease with my family history if I didn't make significant changes. I was definitely looking at medication for high blood pressure and cholesterol. I was looking at heart problems and type 2 diabetes. It was only a matter of time. Now, I've added years of health and vitality to my life. I now make fitness a priority on a daily basis. I have more energy for my family, friends, and work. Along with exercise, my nutrition has changed. I no longer have Ben & Jerry's ice cream on a nightly basis. I'm in the gym regularly. I am also eating salads, vegetables, nuts, and lean meats as I've changed lifelong, unhealthy eating habits.

I have also challenged my own self-sufficiency and isolation problem. I now visit, call, or text three men a day, usually other fathers or close friends. I spent many years without leaning on others. I allowed my tendencies toward self-reliance to have too much control in my life. I want to be clear that my work did not burn me out. I take 100% responsibility for burning myself out. I burned myself out by not loving myself and taking good care of myself in the midst of God's mission for my life. I burned myself out by sitting, consuming sugar, compartment-alizing, isolating, self-centered behaviors, and extreme self-sufficiency. The most important life lesson here is that the will of God never buries us. I did this to myself! Hearing the worst stories of evil, including grotesque acts of sexual abuse, torture, and mutilation, especially those acts toward children, require the greatest level of fitness. For this mission, one has to be spiritually fit, psychologically fit, physically fit, and learn to call upon the fruits of the Holy Spirit on a daily basis. Most importantly, we need other people.

We all need support. We can't let a calloused heart run our lives and households. We can't approach our own emotional pain to isolate ourselves. We all need friends. When I counsel people, I often say two things for both men and women – you need fitness and friends!

Action & Prayer

Solutions have emerged in living a fruitful and vibrant life and being the best version of myself. I now contact three friends per day to stay connected. I have also incorporated social media and screen limits, which keeps me focused on real relationships rather than compartmentalizing, which reinforces unhealthy behaviors and isolation. Regular exercise has given me new opportunities to feel again. Friendships have breathed new life into being able to put forth my best self. The exercise, healthy nutrition, and relationship contacts have helped me to more easily release the burdens I take on in my work life. We must release these burdens at the cross of Christ. These life lessons apply to all parents. Your solutions as a parent include connecting with other parents daily, limiting your social media to stay authentically connected, getting regular exercise, and releasing the burdens that you hold onto with daily increases in trust of the Holy Spirit. The bottom line is that all parents need exercise, nutrition, healthy sleep, screen limits, and friends.

By being the healthiest and best versions of ourselves, we can be our best in remaining restored and free. This gives us our best chance of helping our children live out a life of freedom from the starting line. We want sustained freedom for our children. Yet, they will take on tough stuff in their lives. It is the nature of the journey. We need to seek wisdom as praying parents. "My son, if your heart is wise, My heart will rejoice." (Proverbs 23:15). This devotional is laid out in such a way that it allows us to pray into each of the tough areas that our kids are staring at in their lives. You might be reading this and saying, "It's too late for my son." Well, he may need restoration in Christ. God has no limits. Nothing is impossible for God. There is plenty in this devotional to encourage you toward prayer and sustained prayer that will facilitate freedom and your belief in God's plan for your child.

Other parents starting out strongly want to apply what gives us freedom at the starting line. If that is you, this devotional is also for you. But remember, action is good but praying is better. "I can do all things through Christ who strengthens me" (Philippians 4:13) is more about entering into a golden spot of praying for your children. His strength will sustain you to believe when doubt, concern, oppressing thought patterns, or worry enters in. Trust in God for this situation. God will not waste one second of your child's life. Declare that over each of your children's lives with authority. God loves them and has a plan for their lives. God will use every second.

There are some practical lessons that I learned that brings me to the "action" part of this devotional. The Lord wants us to be smart parents with action, in addition to showing hearts of prayer. As smart parents, we want to impart S.M.A.R.T. living with smart prayer. S.M.A.R.T. involves Securing attachment with our children, Mastering reinforcement for our children, Aiming for Courage in our children, Reclaiming integrity by being present with our children, and instilling a Transforming Vision for each child. S.M.A.R.T. prayer covers these main areas during the 40 days in the most relevant issues of our time as we raise kids in a new era and a new culture with all new challenges.

"Children's children are a crown to the aged, and parents are the pride of their children." (Proverbs 17:6). Think about what makes you the pride of your children. Is it the cars, the houses, the money, and all of the stuff? We know that stuff doesn't last. I have talked with social workers of nursing facilities who have many stories of how adult children are making decisions at the end of Mom's (or Dad's) life that revolve around fighting over money. This seems to be their last-ditch effort to meet unmet needs in their empty hearts.

Is it your achievements that make you the pride of your children? Is it so your child growing up can brag to other children about what you do (i.e., My Dad is a police officer!") or what you've accomplished (i.e., My Mom is an M.D.). Your ability to use your gifts and talents to be used by God to your fullest potential for his Glory is significant for your kids. However, the bottom line is that it's not about what you have (i.e., big house) or what you do (i.e., CEO), but who you are as a mother and a father and how you show up day in and day out in your children's lives.

It is time for us to rise up as brothers and sisters in Christ and take our seat at the table. At the table, parents enter into a lifestyle of prayer for our children. "And he brought them out and said, "Sirs, what must I do to be saved?" So they said, "Believe on the Lord Jesus Christ, and you will be saved, you and your household." Then they spoke the word of the Lord to him and to all who were in his house. And he took them the same hour of the night and washed their stripes. And immediately he and all his family were baptized. Now when he had brought them into his house, he set food before them; and he rejoiced, having believed in God with all his household" (Acts 16:31-34).

DAY 1

Identity

Every child needs to have this question answered, "Who am I?" Identity is your child's perception of themselves. The essence of your child's identity is worth and value. "What am I worth?" "What is my value?" This doesn't just happen because of information processed into the prefrontal cortex. It certainly doesn't happen because of sermons and lectures sitting in school and church. Your child's identity forms over time through extensive conversation, extensive listening, unconditional love, immense affection, grace to fail and compassion after failures, consistent parenting, and deep abiding prayer over time. Identity formation requires perseverance, persistent effort, patience, unconditional love, and attentiveness in our parenting day in and day out. We are building a foundation that involves completely trusting in God. We are trusting in our Lord Jesus Christ and the power of his Holy Spirit to establish a foundation in our son's and daughter's lives that will strengthen, enable, and equip them for a life of victory and freedom.

And let us not grow weary while doing good, for in due season we shall reap if we do not lose heart. Galatians 6:9

My children are "fearfully and wonderfully made" (Psalm 139:14).

Jesus said to him, "'You shall love the Lord your God with all your heart, with all your soul, and with all your mind.' This is the first and great commandment.   And the second is like it: 'You shall love your neighbor as yourself.' (Matthew 22:37-39).

Questions:

How do you talk to your children about their identity?

What aspect of your child's identity do you want to pray into?

What moments in your child's life are the best times for you as a parent to speak into about his or her Godly identity?

Prayer: Lord Jesus, guide my heart as I parent my child's [name each child] identity in God. Speak to my kid(s) about being a masterpiece of your creativity as a son or daughter of the King.

DAY 2

Destiny

Purpose can develop from anything that derives meaning and helps teenagers be a part of something bigger than themselves. This could be spelling bee championships or raising money for a food bank or realizing their passion for medicine. Teenagers can find purpose in seeing injustice in their community and becoming determined that he or she will become a lawyer. Teenagers may realize that they can impact people by the words that they write, so they become determined that they will become a writer. It could be teenagers realizing how important mentors were in their life and decide to become a mentor for elementary kids in academics and or sports. Teenagers are changing the world through inventing things and starting businesses. Below is a great model for self-reflection on finding purpose. Purpose is where your passion, mission, profession, and vocation interconnect.

For purpose to rise, passion for the person of Jesus has to exceed passion for God's vision for your child's life. We do not want our children wrapping their identity in their dreams and what God is calling them to do. First and foremost, identity is in Christ. Identity is in our calling as a son or daughter of God. Destiny is, first and foremost, your child's victorious living that revolves around their relationship with God through Jesus, empowered by the Holy Spirit.

As a parent, this is your #1 priority. For I know the thoughts that I think toward you, says the Lord, thoughts of peace and not of evil, to give you a future and a hope. Then you will call upon Me and go and pray to Me, and I will listen to you. And you will seek Me and find Me, when you search for Me with all your heart. I will be found by you, says the Lord, and I will bring you back from your captivity." (Jeremiah 29:11)

"Seek first the Kingdom of God and his righteousness, and all these things shall be added to you." (Matthew 6:33).

Questions:

What is your child passionate about?

In what ways does your family emphasize that the most important aspect of our destiny is an intimate and close relationship with the Lord?

What are some ways you can foster interests while tapping into conversations about how this fits in with shaping the world for God?

What scripture verses and what blessings can you daily speak over your child and their destiny?

Prayer: Lord, help me to seek you first through prayer. I pray first that my daughter's (son's) purpose will be in you. Second, I pray that you will call her in amazing ways.

DAY 3

Godly Attachments

—————————— ೨ ૭ ೨ ৎ ——————————

Our make up is made of a spirit, a soul which consists of a mind, will, and emotions, and our physical body. It is critical that the Spirit possesses the soul. We want to pray that our children operate out of the Spirit rather than out of the physical body (or flesh). "For those who live according to the flesh set their minds on the things of the flesh, but those who live according to the Spirit, the things of the Spirit." (Romans 8:5).

Every parent will tell you that watching your pre-teen transition into adolescence is a beautiful but messy and complicated process. Moods, psychosexual states, and developmental transitions are exactly that – both messy but beautiful in God's image and perfect planning. Spiritually, our mission is to prayerfully yearn for our kids to operate more and more out of the Spirit.

In psychology, we refer to secure attachment as having strong, healthy relationships with positive, kind, and loving people. The quality of your children's lives is dependent on the quality of their relationships. Of course, first and foremost, we need to pray for their relationship with the Lord. Next, we want to help our kids arrive at Godly attachments – good friends.

"A friend loves at all times, And a brother is born for adversity." (Proverbs 17:17).

"As iron sharpens iron, So a man sharpens the countenance of his friend." (Proverbs 27:17).

Questions:

How satisfied are you with your child's friendships?

What actions can you take to encourage Godliness at the center of those friendships?

When you consider each of your children's friendships, what comes to mind that requires your thoughtful and engaging prayer?

What fruit of the Holy Spirit do you want to pray into your child's relationships?
love, joy, peace, patience, kindness, goodness, faithfulness, gentleness, and self-control.

Prayer: Lord, bless my children with Godly relationships. You are their strength and defense. Bless their Spirits to guide their decisions.

DAY 4

Consistency (8 R's of Consequences)

---·ↄ⌒ↄↄ⌒·---

Our parenting consists of daily pursuing decisions that reflect excellence. Now that we've prayed over identity, destiny, and the critical element of Godly secure attachments guided by the Spirit, let's get into some of the ingredients of parenting day by day. We want to teach obedience and respect for authority. One of the life principles to teach our children is that all actions have consequences.

Healthy parenting involves implementing the 8 R's of Consequences when dealing with behaviors.

1. Release the need for family perfection
2. Realistic expectations; kids will test and learn.
3. Respond, don't react; be relaxed, not angry.
4. Respectful, not shameful

5. Related to the misbehavior (i.e., wash car for car mess)
6. Reasonable in duration, not permanent
7. Revealed in advance: child knows prior to behavior.
8. Restated back to you—showing hearing & listening.

"do not provoke your children to wrath, but bring them up in the training and admonition of the Lord." (Ephesians 6:4).

"He who keeps instruction is in the way of life, But he who refuses correction goes astray." (Proverbs 10:17).

Questions:

How might you apply the 8 R's of consequences into your correcting with love?

Some error on the side of mercy. Others error on the side of "too much" discipline. What comes to mind as you balance nurturing with consistency?

What are your three favorite scripture verses when it comes to parenting and love?

Prayer: Lord, bless my children and form their character that brings glory to you!

DAY 5

Speak Good and Maturity into Future

As parents, we need to recognize the importance of what we believe in shaping situations. Parents need to shape situations and their responses to them under the direction of the Holy Spirit. Parents can plant godly seeds and reap godly harvests by speaking goodness into the lives of their children. We can plant "thought" seeds that can profoundly affect children's reality. We need to speak good into our children. "For as he thinks in his heart, so is he." (Proverbs 23:7).

Parents need to take time to honor their kids, speak good into them, express belief in who they are, remind them of their resilience in overcoming difficulties, and communicate victory in their life.

"But you are a chosen generation, a royal priesthood, a holy nation, His own special people, that you may proclaim the praises of Him who called you out of darkness into His marvelous light" (1 Peter 2:9).

35

"You are great in counsel and mighty in work, for your eyes are open to all the ways of the sons of men, to give everyone according to his ways and according to the fruit of his doings." (Jeremiah 32:19).

Questions:

How can you bless your children's future more?

How do you want to speak differently after reading this entry?

Which scripture verse can you speak out loud daily this week as you pray into your child's future? Declare a great future for your child, out loud with faith.

Prayer: Holy Spirit, illuminate my mind with revelation in hearing, discerning, speaking, and ministering to my children about their gifts, talents, beauty, words, and value.

DAY 6

Temper & Anger

⸻ ೨ᏩᏩ᠖ ⸻

Anger is a huge issue when raising kids, especially boys. Did you grow up with an angry parent or with angry parents? Did you experience anger in rages, hatred, aggression, and abuse? Were you frightened growing up? Were you hurt and always feeling like you were walking on eggshells? If this is you, you need some deep healing from soul/spirit hurts. You need healing from your trauma. You can break ancestral lines with deep forgiveness, but not at the surface level. You can break strongholds in your life with repentance, forgiveness, and deliverance, but only if it happens in the spirit of healing. God can touch these hurts in your life, and the blood of Jesus gives freedom.

One of the awesome things about ending anger is bringing the "passing down" to a halt at this generation. Your kids can be the first generation of a new family line rooted in peace rather than anger. This can be a tremendous blessing and an amazing inheritance, perhaps only second to helping them know the Lord Jesus personally.

"A fool vents all his feelings, But a wise man holds them back." (Proverbs 29:11).

"for the wrath of man does not produce the righteousness of God." (James 1:20).

"The discretion of a man makes him slow to anger, And his glory is to overlook a transgression." (Proverbs 19:11).

Questions:

Is there a soul / Spirit hurt from the past that comes up for you? Take your time and write this hurt out. Pray for the Holy Spirit to breathe healing into this event in your life.

What scripture comes to mind as you speak peace into the anger in your life, your co-parent's life, or your child's life?

What thought patterns that fuel anger require your repentance? Are there thoughts of resentment, bitterness, or divisiveness? Go to God and ask him for your forgiveness. Reflect on this process here.

Prayer: Dear Jesus, move me through the healing process so I can enter more fully into a life-giving relationship that the Lord has for me. I declare that you are the healer, and you can get rid of the hindrances and blocks to the fullness of the Holy Spirit. And may this healing encourage my walk with my children, so they will only experience calm from me.

DAY 7

Temper & Anger Versus Peace

—————— ༄༅༅ ——————

First and foremost, parents need to seek the Lord. Out of our relationship with the Lord Jesus, our spirit can possess our soul. Out of our relationship with the Lord Jesus, we are led by the Holy Spirit. When we listen to our spirit, our inward man, we can deal with our own temper and tendency toward anger. There are a lot of feelings that we experience as parents: the anger category consists of aggravation, disappointment, intolerance, irritability, feuding, frustration, hatred, hostility, resentment, retaliation, revenge, and temper tantrums. Tantrums? Yes, parents have tantrums. When the Holy Spirit leads us, we mature and respond calmly under pressure.

Then there is dealing with your kids—the following techniques diffuse temper reactions, over-reactions, and explosive behaviors.

- Stay CALM: Calmly breathe, Attend to the present, Let go of perfections, Mindful of the moment.
- When discussing issues, Be CLEAR: Clarify, Listen, Evaluate, Address differences, and Reinforce specifically & carefully in conversation.
- Trust in God during disagreements and when hearing difficult tones.

"So then, my beloved brethren, let every man be swift to hear, slow to speak, slow to wrath; for the wrath of man does not produce the righteousness of God." (James 1:19-20).

Questions:

How can you let the Holy Spirit lead you when you deal with a child's overreaction?

What does it look like for your family members to become slow to anger?

How can CALM help you engage more in your relationship with Jesus? Calmly breathe, Attend to the present, Let Go of Perfections, and be Mindful of what God is doing?

Prayer: Lord, bless my children with the peace of Jesus Christ!

DAY 8

PRAISE

Children need encouragement and praise. It is important to praise effort: "I liked the way you didn't give up on that task." It is important to praise reflection: "I like your thinking as you consider alternative strategies." It is important to praise your child's focus on solutions: "I just love the way you are approaching this problem, and you came up with a great solution." It is important to praise strategic thinking, "I really like your plan in preparing for the exam." It is also important to praise their expression, "I really appreciate how you expressed your feelings at dinner this evening."

"he who exhorts, in exhortation; he who gives, with liberality; he who leads, with diligence; he who shows mercy, with cheerfulness." (Romans 12:8).

Questions:

In what ways is praising your children pleasing to God?

What specific effort can you praise your child today with eye contact, smiling, and delivering your praise in a very specific way?

What three things can I praise in my children today?

Prayer: Lord, as you renew my mind, I ask you to give me the grace to cooperate with you fully in the process of encouraging my children without hesitation. I submit myself to my calling as an encourager on the authority of and in the name of Jesus Christ. Amen!

DAY 9

Building Optimism and Hope

Building optimism is best started early. It is also never too late to start building optimism. Optimism is a way of thinking. Optimism is not overly positive thinking like pilots saying, "we don't need to de-ice the planes." No, we want responsible thinking. Optimism is not ignoring important feelings like sadness after getting cut from tryouts. No, we want emotionally intelligent thinking. Expressing our feelings is important in healthy families.

Optimism is seeing bad events as empowering. Optimism is bouncing back after setbacks. Optimism is seeing the possibility in the face of adversity. Optimism is seeing problems not as permanent, but temporary. Optimism is seeing problems not as pervasive, but specific.

"For there is hope for a tree, If it is cut down, that it will sprout again, And that its tender shoots will not cease." (Job 14:7).

"Be of good courage, And He shall strengthen your heart, All you who hope in the Lord." (Psalm 31:24).

Questions:

What problem in my child's life can I see as temporary, not permanent?

What area in my child's life do I need to pray hope into?

In what way does the Lord want me to be more optimistic? How does this apply to my faith?

Prayer: Lord, give me your possibility thinking. Give me optimism in the face of adversity. Give me your hope to see how you see. I break any agreements with old ways of thinking. Old things pass away, behold, give me your thinking, your optimism and your hope.

DAY 10

Storytelling

Reflective parents can identify (1) most embarrassing moments, (2) favorite achievements, (3) most distressing experiences, (4) moments of breakthrough, (5) conflicts with friends, (6) relationship hardships, (7) great and not-so-great moments with teachers, (8) and the ups and downs of many of their childhood years and grade levels in school through childhood and adolescence. Some people tell themselves they have a "bad memory." If this is you, turn to the Lord and ask Him to renew your mind and ask for grace to cooperate with the process of being renewed in Christ. His grace is enough. And, if you've had a traumatic brain injury (TBI), his healing and grace is still enough.

- For most people, it simply takes time and reflectiveness. The goal is to share your life with your kid. Reading and story-telling are 100% more substantially meaningful than TV before bed.

- As tweens transition, teenagers don't need parents to be PREACHY! Instead, they need parents to be VULNERABLE!
- Authentic connection involves vulnerability, not guarded lessons that reflect "I told you so" types of expressions.
- Story-telling is about timing.

"On the same day Jesus went out of the house and sat by the sea. And great multitudes were gathered together to Him, so that He got into a boat and sat; and the whole multitude stood on the shore. Then He spoke many things to them in parables, saying: "Behold, a sower went out to sow. And as he sowed......'" (Matthew 13:1-4).

Questions:

When you were your child's age and the current school grade, what key stories do you recall that capture your reflectiveness?

What are some of your embarrassing moment stories that you can share with your kids? In what ways can you help them be unafraid of embarrassment?

In what ways can you be less preachy and more vulnerable with your kids? Were you ever scared? What helped you not be scared?

Prayer: Lord, I pray for vulnerability and reflectiveness. I declare that the Spirit of the Lord is upon me that I may share my life.

DAY 11

Sexual Purity

Sexual purity in the Lord is possible and attainable. While we may battle with temptation and have to say "No" to the flesh all the days of our lives, in Jesus Christ, through victory from his blood, by the word of God, by his Holy Spirit, we have been equipped in such a way that we can live lives that honor the Lord. We can live lives that are pure, holy, and honorable. This only happens with a life depending on the Lord Jesus. We have to be mindful of these things when considering purity for our kids. Our kids need a life that depends on the Lord for small and big things. While he might be focusing on making that team, you are also praying for his spirit to bring light and purity with his friends.

Your children are growing up in a generation like no other. Today, 7-year-olds are exposed to pornography. Children as young as 9 or 10 learn the relative health risks of anal vs. oral vs. vaginal intercourse. Very young pre-teens are sexting each other. First graders are receiving condoms. Healthy young men cannot perform without

Viagra because of porn addiction. Two in five sexually active teen girls have an STD. The sexual revolution has brought warped mental and spiritual faculties.

The only way our children don't get run over by this culture and are victims of the sexual anarchy is with a relationship with Jesus. The only way to flourish and thrive is to live a radical lifestyle that is in sharp contrast from the life our culture reinforces. Our culture reinforces immediate gratification. In the Kingdom of God, we have completely different values.

"For the eyes of the Lord run to and fro throughout the whole earth, to show Himself strong on behalf of those whose heart is loyal to Him." (2 Chronicles 16:9).

Questions:

In what ways have you communicated the three fundamental lessons of sexuality for children: sexual union exists (1) to make babies, (2) to nurture Mom and Dad's love, (3) and direct us back to the love of the Father, Son, and Holy Spirit?

How can you help your children counter-cultural messages about sexuality and engage in teachable moments (i.e., a lewd advertisement at a mall or a sensual song while sitting in a restaurant)?

In what ways can you maintain ongoing discussions (versus one talk only) as you develop their character traits to be good stewards of their sexuality and develop their patience, self-control, and integrity in all aspects of their lives?

Prayer: Lord, I pray that my kids can live with such wholehearted devotion that the Lord will show himself strong on our behalf. I pray that our kids can live a life completely sold out to the power of Jesus, whose grace will anoint and bless a life of purity.

DAY 12

Family Dinner Conversations

---∂◌∂⊂---

The success of a family depends on the success of your bonding. The best predictor of a healthy bonding family is a family who has dinners together. A great place to start is a minimum of four dinners per week together. It helps if parents can plan ahead on conversations. The sun/storm/rainbow technique can assist with daily reflection and bonding and provide deliberate reminiscing and savoring the moments. Each evening, a family member can share their experiences of the day with the sun-storm-rainbow technique. The Sun is something that delighted you that day. The Storm is something that challenged you that day. The Rainbow is something positive you learned about yourself or discovered in the storm. By reflecting with the sun-storm-rainbow, individuals increase their reflectiveness, cultivate reminiscing opportunities, and increase gratitude.

"Then our mouth was filled with laughter, And our tongue with singing. Then they said among the nations, "The Lord has done great things for them." (Psalm 126: 2).

Questions:

How satisfied are you with the frequency of family dinners? Is the dinner a family priority?

In what ways can you prepare for the family dinner during the key window of learning and connection that happens during the dinner?

How can you apply the sun-storm-rainbow technique into tonight's dinner?

Prayer: Lord, I pray that our family can laugh with each other rather than at each other. I pray that our family can honor each other, build each other up, and our dinners can be a source of joy and encouragement.

DAY 13

Managing Media Exposure (Social Media)

Children are growing up as digital natives. Two-year-old's are being babysat by cell phones. Teens are refusing to go on cruises because they don't want to disrupt their Snapchat streaks. Kids are stealing their parents' credit cards to buy likes (e.g., social media posts). Cousins seeing each other at family reunions are texting each other, standing a few feet apart. Families at Disney World are sitting on a train, and all members are staring at the phone rather than mindfully enjoying the sights and sounds of a dream vacation. Teen boys are growing up as video game addicts with limited social skills. Teen girls are having panic attacks as they cope with cyberbullying.

The answer to all of this is having a family mission to do things differently than the culture. Parents need a plan. Some parents prohibit social media until college and teens are content; they don't believe they are missing anything. Parents use rating systems from dove and common sense media for TV and movies. Parents use parental controls for TikTok. Some parents have no TV's. Some parents have limits on video games for boys; others have no video games. Parents need a supervisory plan on YouTube, Hulu, and phone time. In addition to a "PLAN," parents need to encourage regular conversation on restraint, authentic connecting, and being wise.

Restraint

"He who has knowledge spares his words, And a man of understanding is of a calm spirit." (Proverbs 17:27).

Authentic Connecting Over Isolation

"A man who isolates himself seeks his own desire; He rages against all wise judgment." (Proverbs 18:1).

Social Media Posting with Discernment

"A fool has no delight in understanding, But in expressing his own heart." (Proverbs 18:2).

Questions:

What is your family digital plan?

What are some ways you can engage in ongoing conversations about restraint, authentic connecting, and posting with discernment?

How can you convey that the quality of relationships in a person is your family's highest value?

Prayer: Lord, I pray for wisdom for limits and wisdom with media.

DAY 14

Trust in God

───────────── ༄ ༅ ༆ ─────────────

Teaching our children to trust in God is a balance of faith and problem-solving. Identifying the worries is the first step; not so easy. But, awareness of consciousness is power. Anything we focus on expands in our consciousness. When we focus on the person of Jesus Christ, his presence expands in our consciousness. What has been expanding in your conscience? What do you worry about the most? Problem-solving is the second step. The opposite of worry is problem-solving. Ranking worries from least to most distressing can be a helpful strategy. The main goal is to identify worries and brainstorm solutions to those worries. Parents can make a difference in brainstorming three to five possible solutions for their kids' worries. Sometimes, empowerment occurs when the worries are categorized into those things in your child's control (i.e., preparing for the spelling test) and those things outside of control (i.e., making the basketball team).

"There is no fear in love; but perfect love casts out fear because fear involves torment. But he who fears has not been made perfect in love." (1 John 4:18).

"And which of you by worrying can add one cubit to his stature? If you then are not able to do the least, why are you anxious for the rest? Consider the lilies, how they grow: they neither toil nor spin; and yet I say to you, even Solomon in all his glory was not arrayed like one of these. If then God so clothes the grass, which today is in the field and tomorrow is thrown into the oven, how much more will He clothe you, O you of little faith? And do not seek what you should eat or what you should drink, nor have an anxious mind." (Luke 12:25-29).

Questions:

What in our family needs to get handed over to the Lord?

What fears do you hold as a parent that need to get replaced with faith? Speak those fears out loud, followed by the truth of Jesus and scripture to counter those fears?

What do I need to trust you more for in our children's life?

Prayer: Lord, I pray for the end of worry in this family. Because we are united with Christ and sit with him in heavenly places, I renounce and cancel every worry that comes our way. I declare our family as completely signed over and sealed by our Lord Jesus Christ.

65

DAY 15

Building a Family Culture of Honor

Establishing a culture of honor prior to teenage years makes a difference. The way to prevent children from becoming embittered, hardened, and distant is by sowing into our children the capacity to express fondness and gratitude. Honoring each other will pay huge dividends. And, it is never too late to start pearl finding. One practical way this is handled is by honoring a ritual that can make a huge difference for families. In a culture of honor, brothers and sisters are trained to honor their siblings on birthdays. As they do, practice will accelerate their pearl finding skills. Over time, a family culture of honor deepens with love, respect, and expressing goodness over time.

"Be kindly affectionate to one another with brotherly love, in honor giving preference to one another" Romans 12:10).

Questions:

On this upcoming birthday, what specific way can I honor my child? Is it his Wisdom: Creativity, Curiosity, Good Judgment & Critical Thinking, Love of Learning, Perspective & Sharing Wisdom?

Is it her Courage: Bravery & Valor, Perseverance & Persistence, Honesty / Authenticity & Integrity, Zeal / Enthusiasm & Vigor?

Is it his Interpersonal Skills: Love & Valuing Close Relationships, Sharing & Caring, Kindness / Generosity / Nurturance & Niceness – doing favors and good deeds; & Social and Emotional Intelligence?

Is it his sense of Justice: Teamwork & Loyalty, Fairness, and Leadership?

Is it her Temperance: Forgiveness, Humility, Prudence, & Self-Regulation / Self-Control?
Is it his Transcendence: Appreciation of Beauty and Excellence [Awe, Wonder] and Noticing Excellence in Others, Gratitude, Hope, Optimism, Humor, and Playfulness; Spirituality [Faith & Purpose]?

And what stories or examples do I want to highlight from this past year as I honor my son or daughter with immense passion and honor?
How can I honor the Lord by honoring the very best in my son or daughter?

Prayer: Lord, I pray for an awareness of your presence in this home. I pray that this family will honor you by our love and honor of each other. Lord Jesus, facilitate a culture of honor in this home.

DAY 16

Humility

---∂૬∂૬---

We live in a culture of self-obsession. Our son likes to joke that more people die from selfies than shark attacks (actually true). Teens are growing up in a generation of self-absorption. Social media reinforces a narcissistic attitude.

Reinforcing a culture of honor is one of the answers for your family in differentiating from the self-obsession culture. Family conversations about shaping the culture gets the focus off of ourselves and onto something valued that is bigger than us. But it is the day in and day out conversations about the value of humility that makes the biggest difference. When discussing arguments or preventing pride, humility is one of the greatest goals for character development.

"Be completely humble and gentle; be patient, bearing with one another in love" (Ephesians 4:2, NIV).

"Humble yourselves in the sight of the Lord, and he will lift you up" (James 4:10).

"The fear of the Lord is the instruction of wisdom, And before honor is humility." (Proverbs 15:33).

"By humility and the fear of the Lord are riches and honor and life." (Proverbs 22:4).

Questions:

How can you help convey humility while helping your children listen with humility to biblical instruction and correction?

How can you help your child seek to humbly show preference to their siblings over their own desires?

How can you, as the parent, convey the process of humbling ourselves before the Lord? How often do you say "I am sorry" for overreacting, being impatient, or having an anger reaction?

Prayer: Lord, I pray for the gift of humility to shine in this family. Jesus, may your radical love transform our very being, from the inside out. Infuse within our very core, a deep and abiding humility that is evident to all, for your Glory.

DAY 17

Unconditional Love

Unconditional love parenting can be taught to children early on, and serve as a reminder to us that this is a value to the family. When a child being roughhoused by a sibling says, "I don't love you." He can be taught, In our family, we always love each other, and we never say, "I don't love you." Instead, when you get pinned down by your brother, you can say, "I am angry at you when you hold me down." As a family, we can teach our children that love for each other never changes on the whim or by a recent argument or fight. Instead, expressing anger appropriately is valued and respected in our family.

The best environment for a child to thrive is one that is grounded in unconditional love. Unconditional love parenting is rooted in the principle that there is nothing a child can do to increase your love for them. Additionally, there is nothing a child can do to decrease your love for them.

Sometimes our own blind spots cause conditional love parenting.

These underlying issues get in the way of loving our children unconditionally. These issues may be anger, unresolved hurts from the past, or resentments and subsequent unforgiveness, to name a few.

"Who can understand his errors? Cleanse me from secret faults. Keep back your servant also from presumptuous sins; let them not have dominion over me. Then I shall be blameless, and I shall be innocent of great transgression." (Psalm 19:12-13).

Questions:

What are some ways that you can express your unconditional love to your children?

Is there a particular achievement that you want your child to very much accomplish? Does this get in the way of unconditional acceptance and approval?

What are your blind spots that God needs to touch and create within you a new heart?

Prayer: Lord, look deep within me. Reveal to me any hidden conditions. Speak to my mind, move in my heart, and bring radical changes to my inner being. Bring forth a parent who loves unconditionally, in Jesus's name!

DAY 18

Gratitude

───────────⟋⟋───────────

One way to build gratitude in families is by applying gratitude at family dinner time. Every dinner, family members identify something that they are grateful for. This can be interwoven with the "three good things" technique, in which each night, family members journal three things that they are grateful for.

Every Sunday, the family can identify one person in their family's life who has made a difference and had a positive impact on one or more family members. The family takes 15 minutes to write a letter to this person or makes a video or posts something about this person. Grateful parents lead their families by incorporating expressions of gratitude when honoring a child, writing specific reasons for gratefulness, writing gratitude letters, and increasing consciousness in word choices. Grateful parents use gratitude words such as "blessed," "those were blessings," "fortunate," "appreciative," "obliged," "thankful," and "prosperous."

"All this is for your benefit, so that the grace that is reaching more and more people may cause thanksgiving to overflow to the glory of God" (2 Corinthians 4:15, NIV).

"My counsel for you is simple and straightforward: Just go ahead with what you've been given. You received Christ Jesus, the Master; now live him. You're deeply rooted in him. You're well constructed upon him. You know your way around the faith. Now do what you've been taught. School's out; quit studying the subject and start living it! And let your living spill over into thanksgiving" (Colossians 2:6-7, The Message).

"Continue earnestly in prayer, being vigilant in it with thanksgiving" (Colossians 4:2).

Questions:

In the Spirit of Psalm 77, what are three specific memories that you would describe as wonders of the Lord in your life?

What gratitude exercise or method can you implement with your family?

How can a gratitude lifestyle be incorporated into your life so that thanksgiving can overflow to the glory of God?

Prayer: Lord, move in my Spirit to overflow with gratitude. I give thanks to you, Lord, with all my heart; I will tell of all your wonderful deeds. I will not let a day go by without my children hearing me, thank you. Bless this commitment, in Jesus's name.

DAY 19

Prayer Life

———————— ༄ ༅ ༄ ————————

There is nothing more important that we can do in life than pray. Prayer is the most effective ministry in our lives. The power of prayer is limitless. All things are possible for those who believe. Assuming we are taking care of our responsibilities, is there anything more important than prayer? You can have a burden to solve problems at work, to minister to others, and to take care of our children (i.e., clean, cook, laundry, shop). In all that we do, it is easy to forget that everything flows out of prayer. Prayer is about intimacy. Prayer is about our relationship with God and falling more in love with God, knowing him, and being known by him.

In addition to our love relationship with the Lord, it is critical that we also recognize that prayer changes things. Prayer produces results. Prayer is about caring for souls. Prayer pushes back demonic oppression. Prayer changes ungodly beliefs into Godly beliefs. Prayer is going to the Lord and asking the Lord. Some things don't happen unless we ask.

"Lord, teach us to pray...he said to them, 'When you pray, say: 'Our Father in heaven, Hallowed be your name. Your kingdom come. Your will be done on earth as it is in heaven. Give us day by day our daily bread. And forgive us our sins, for we also forgive everyone who is indebted to us. And do not lead us into temptation, but deliver us from the evil one" (Luke 11:1-4).

"I have set watchmen on your walls, O Jerusalem; they shall never hold their peace day or night. You who make mention of the Lord, do not keep silent, and give him no rest till he establishes and till he makes Jerusalem a praise in the earth" (Isaiah 62: 6-7).

Questions:

Which scripture verse can you speak out loud over the life of your child?

When do you fast and pray for your children? No better time than now. "Return to me with all your heart, with fasting and weeping and mourning" (Joel 2:12).

In what way are you a watchman for your family? What areas do you need to look out for as you pray for the kids – more unselfishness, looking out for your sibling more, more responsibility in chores, more discipline in school work….. What areas in the lives of your children require more focused prayer?

Prayer: Lord, as a watchman for my family, I pray that prayer will be a life habit for everyone in my family. I pray that we can have maximum focus on you, Jesus. Without wavering, let us pray effectively and not grow weary as we experience prayer that produces results.

DAY 20

Video Game Awareness

---------⌒ↄᏬↄϲ⌒---------

Parents need to know that video game use can easily lead to video game addiction. I recently sat with a 9-year old boy who started crying and pulled his shirt over his head simply because I suggested to his mother that he needed to limit the use of video games. A college friend contacted me about her 11-year old son whose aggressive behaviors elevate when he is requested to turn off the system. The HPA/HPG pathways pump adrenalin, cortisol, and testosterone into the bloodstream, causing problems. Digital media such as video games work through the visual system to reprogram the brain via neuronal plasticity, leading to aggression, increased sexual behaviors, back-talking, concentration problems, and a range of behavior problems. Parents need wisdom when dealing with digital media. For sexual purity, parents need to use tools like covenant eyes; they need to lock down all devices with passwords. A good rule is limiting smartphones until at least age 14, but possibly 18. Another good rule is no social media until age 18. Also, no devices or TV's in bedrooms.

"Don't turn your back on wisdom, for she will protect you. Love her, and she will guard you" (Proverbs 4:6, NIV).

"If any of you lacks wisdom, let him ask of God, who gives to all liberally and without reproach, and it will be given to him." (James 1:5).

Questions:

What is a Godly perspective when it comes to digital exposure for your children? And how does being in the world but not of it fit on this topic?

If you have not implemented video game limits, why haven't you? What limits can you incorporate now to help your children, particularly boys, learn moderation, patience, and personal responsibility? This includes video games but also includes handheld devices.

What healthy Spirit-led sports, activities, or games can your family implement as stress reduction behaviors and family relationship building besides screen time?

Prayer: Lord, as a watchman for my family, I pray for the wisdom to deal with these real-life issues like video games and digital media with common sense, Godly perspective, and wisdom from heaven.

DAY 21

Education

---------------◦⟨◦⟨---------------

When it comes to education, the mission is to help our children love to learn. First and foremost, the objective of education is to become a better human being. The virtue of wisdom consists of the following strengths: creativity, curiosity, good judgment, critical thinking, taking perspective, sharing wisdom, knowledge, and the love of learning.

Love of learning is more important than grades. In our family, we've gone through seasons when we haven't even looked at our children's report cards. Love of learning is also more important than test results. It is very common for parents to be concerned, worried, or influenced about results from Iowa testing (ITBS), TerraNova testing, preliminary SAT or National Merit Scholarship Qualifying Testing (NMSQT), or SAT scores. Results from IQ tests (Stanford-Binet, WAIS, WISC, etc.) and achievement tests (WIAT, Kaufman, Woodcock-Johnson) do not replace LOVE OF LEARNING. Parents need to strengthen themselves in the truth of God.

Numbers do not determine your child's future. Love of learning is the best educational predictor.

"A disciple is not above his teacher, but everyone who is perfectly trained will be like his teacher" (Luke 6:40).

"Give *instruction* to a wise *man,* and he will be still wiser; Teach a just *man,* and he will increase in learning." (Proverbs 9:9).

Questions:

How can I reach out to my children's teachers and express gratitude and be a positive in their life?

How can I foster curiosity in my child? What one new idea or conversation can we have at our family dinner today?

What questions can I ask my children today that will promote and reinforce the love of learning?

Prayer: Lord, I pray that you bless my children with creativity, curiosity, and good judgment. Bless them with critical thinking, wisdom, and love of learning. Holy Spirit, illuminate knowledge for your Glory.

DAY 22

Politeness

Good manners and politeness are jewels for a family. Ideally, our family members are known for their manners and politeness. Regardless of personality, temperament, or communication style, good etiquette builds bonds and connections. We want our children to be known by their teachers, neighbors, aunts and uncles, grandparents, and friends by their politeness. "I'm sorry," "I appreciate you," "Please, may I," "Thank you," "You're welcome," "Thanks so much..." Parents want to communicate expectations and standards for dining, conversation and attire.

"In your hearts revere Christ as Lord. Always be prepared to give an answer to everyone who asks you to give the reason for the hope that you have. But do this with gentleness and respect" (1 Peter 3:15, NIV).

"Do not be deceived: 'evil company corrupts good habits" (1 Corinthians 15:33).

"Let the words of my mouth and the meditation of my heart be acceptable in your sight, O Lord, my strength and my redeemer" (Psalm 19:14).

"The merciful man does good for his own soul, but he who is cruel troubles his own flesh" (Proverbs 11:17).

Questions:

What can I do today to talk with the children about polite behaviors?

How can I incorporate politeness during the process of discipline? How can I make a commitment today to incorporate my manners and politeness during the course of heated exchanges with children?

In what way does my family honor the Lord with politeness?

Prayer: Lord, I pray for your guidance as we instruct our children on how we can reflect the light and salt of God through our manners and politeness.

DAY 23

Sibling Rivalry

There are many things about the parenting process that can be summarized by being inconvenienced. Sometimes, during low moments, parents can feel like it is "all" about being inconvenienced. During our high moments, we realize it is all worth it. Excellent parents can tolerate inconveniences with poise. I call the process of repeatedly being inconvenienced with more understanding as increasing the tolerance threshold. The goal isn't to pull up the bootstraps and force ourselves through yet "another difficulty." Instead, the growth of our tolerance threshold should bring us to a place of being able to nurture fondness more effectively, cultivate an attitude of gratitude more regularly, and genuinely express good-hearted positivity. Sibling rivalry is one of those very difficult inconveniences because they touch on the core of our family – a desire for deeply close bonds.

We need to fight off those tendencies toward thinking we are helpless in these situations. When in doubt, call a family meeting. "Listen, this is how we treat each other."

"We look out for each other." If there is a disagreement, allow family members to talk it out at the meeting one person at a time. If there is a spiritual attack, we need to remember that believers have power, authority, and protection (Luke 10:17-19). "Let's come together and pray against a spirit of disunity. We are bonded in Christ!"

"How wonderful, how beautiful, when brothers and sisters get along! It's like costly anointing oil flowing down Aaron's beard, flowing down the collar of his priestly robes. It's like the dew on Mouth Hermon flowing down the slopes of Zion. Yes, that's where God commands the blessing, ordains eternal life" (Psalm 133:1-3, The Message).

Questions:

How can you promote sibling connection more than competition?

What are some specific areas in your child's life in which prayer can be focused on? Is it more kindness, more empathy & compassion, more patience, or deeper understanding?

What kinds of conversations can you explore at dinner time to promote unity and bridge-building as opposed to divisiveness and disunity?

Prayer: Lord, I pray for the patience to nurture fondness amongst family relationships. I pray for the spiritual sensitivity to be on guard (1 Peter 5:8). I pray that each family member is aware of Satan's schemes, snares and devices (2 Corinthians 2:11). We proclaim our victory in Jesus Christ.

DAY 24

Fitness & Sports

"Get outside and play." No TV, clear limits on video games, and clear limits on smartphones and tablets. This is a good start. But the second-best gift a kid can receive is hearing the words "Get outside and play." On the one hand, one of the stressors young people face is the over-scheduling of sports in their lives. On the other hand, schools are cutting gym and recess while screen time has amplified in quantity and quality. Nearly one in three kids or teens are overweight or obese.

When I was growing up in Bolingbrook, Illinois, many of us kids would meet out front on Churchill Drive and pick teams for our basketball, football, baseball, soccer, and wiffleball games. I'll never forget the fun I had with so many friends. When teams were picked, Todd was always chosen last because he was the least skilled. In the current generation, while the better athletes are primarily participating in traveling teams, the Todd's in neighborhoods across the country are playing video games.

The best gift a kid can receive is hearing the words, "Let's get outside and play," and the parent joins in. Family needs to play together—King ball tag, wiffleball, kickball, freeze tag, basketball, soccer, you name it. Let's do it!

"Therefore, whether you eat or drink, or whatever you do, do all to the glory of God" (1 Corinthians 10:31).

"For physical training is of some value, but godliness has value for all things, holding promise for both the present *life and the life to come" (1 Timothy 4:8, NIV).*

Questions:

What changes do you need to make so you can model optimal fitness for our children?

What kinds of sporting events and family activities can your family incorporate into your routine?

What scriptures support your family's goals of optimal nutrition and exercise?

Prayer: Lord, I pray for balance and fun for our family. Remind us regularly of the importance of playing outside together as a family. Give us balanced nutrition with sugar intake limits. Give us sports opportunities outside as a family. May we play with great sportsmanship and have fun exercising together for the Glory of God.

DAY 25

Excellence in Sleep Patterns

Let's clarify the recommendations for each of the age groups by the American Academy of Pediatrics (AAP). The following sleep per 24 hours is recommended to promote optimal health:

- Infants 4 months to 12 months should sleep 12 to 16 hours.
- Children 1 to 2 years of age should sleep 11 to 14 hours.
- Children 3 to 5 years of age should sleep 10 to 13 hours.
- Children 6 to 12 years of age should sleep 9 to 12 hours.
- Teenagers 13 to 18 years of age should sleep 8 to 10 hours.

It is common for parents to have the number "8" in their memory and apply for that number when scheduling bedtime. This is a problem. Your restless and hyperactive 7-year old may be experiencing 4-5 fewer hours of sleep than they should be getting. Look, we are quick to make sure our child takes his antibiotic, but we ignore the need for sleep. And this includes us parents. As a nation, we are sleep deprived. Our families need more sleep.

"And suddenly a great tempest arose on the sea, so that the boat was covered with the waves. But he was asleep" (Matthew 8:24).

"It is vain for you to rise up early, to sit up late, to eat the bread of sorrows; for so he gives his beloved sleep" (Psalm 127:2).

Questions:

On issues like this, parents often feel helpless about the schedules and routines. What are some ways that you can reverse helplessness and assert authority over this area with parental warmth?

Teens rarely get 6 hours of sleep on weekdays. We know lack of sleep can limit teen's ability to problem solve, learn, reason, focus, listen, and engage. How can you incorporate prayer into the ways you educate your teens on the value of sleep?

Prayer around your house can declare sweet sleep. Do you ever walk around your house and pray for the Glory of God and God's sweet spirit to be in our children's sweet sleep?

Prayer: Lord, I pray for the wisdom to re-evaluate what we are doing in this family. Help me with our sleep schedules and give us the grace to make changes that bring more rest for our family.

DAY 26

Healthy Nutrition

∂૭૯

We often separate church from work or the gospel from our daily life. Christ needs to be a part of everything we do. Greater is he who is in me than he who is in the world. Where I go, the Holy Spirit goes. So this is the reason the Big 3 of behavioral health is in this devotional. We want the Lord to bless our fitness (and fun), sleep, and nutrition. We don't want to live compartmentalized lives. We want to involve the Holy Spirit in all that we do. Christ is in us, the hope of Glory. The Kingdom of God is within us. We want to regularly consult with the Lord as he is our all in all. And this includes our nutrition.

We eat to live rather than live to eat. For those who are addicted to Oreo's, Ben & Jerry's, and M&M's, we need to recognize that this is not fueling your bodies. Instead, this sugar is squelching your body from real fuel. More than 100 million Americans have diabetes or prediabetes. Added sugars should be parents' primary concern for their children. The most common added sugars are regular table sugar (sucrose) and high-fructose corn syrup. The average intake is approximately 77 grams of added sugar per day. According to the American Heart Association (AHA), children ages 2 to 18 years should have less than 25 grams of sugar per day.

"Do you not know that those who run in a race all run, but one receives the prize? Run in such a way that you may obtain it. And everyone who competes *for the prize* is temperate in all things. Now they *do it* to obtain a perishable crown, but we *for* an imperishable *crown.* Therefore I run thus: not with uncertainty. Thus I fight: not as *one who* beats the air. But I discipline my body and bring *it* into subjection, lest, when I have preached to others, I myself should become disqualified" (1 Corinthians 9:24-27).

Questions:

One of the issues here is to grow self-control and self-discipline. The solutions are prayer and action. How can you call upon God for the fruit of self-control in the life of your family?

Nutrition conversation starts with stress reduction. From Ben & Jerry's to French silk pie, tension reduction behaviors often include food. How can we begin to teach our children that food is fuel rather than stress reduction?

One of the best predictors of family success is family dinners. Have you ever taken the time to ask God to bless your family dinners? Have you ever taken time to pray for God to move in your family with revelation, wisdom, understanding, love, consideration, politeness, and mercy during our family dinners?

Prayer: Lord, I pray for self-discipline for each family member. I pray that you will lead us to fuel our bodies with good nutrition. Help us seek you and healthy strategies when coping with stress. Eliminate the mindset that food is our reward. You are our reward.

DAY 27

Good Friends

Sociological studies suggest that humans are hard-wired to seek and make friends in ways we have always done in the past, regardless of new social network opportunities such as Instagram, Facebook, Twitter, Snapchat, and Tumblr. In an analysis of college students and Hadza hunter-gatherers of Tanzania, teenagers and young adults have hard-wired similarities. Networks consist of one or two best friends, friendships in a "friend group" of five to six close friends, and placed within a broader group of approximately 150 people. While the communication methods between friends have changed, the development of friend networks appears to have remained similar throughout history.

This remains an area of prayer for every parent. We want to pray for our children to carefully discern who is a good friend. We want our children to be surrounded by Godly people who they can give to and receive from in healthy ways.

"Therefore, as the elect of God, holy and beloved, put on tender mercies, kindness, humility, meekness, longsuffering; bearing with one another, and forgiving one another, if anyone has a complaint against another; even as Christ forgave you, so you also must do. But above all these things put on love, which is the bond of perfection." (Colossians 3:12-14).

Questions:

Which friends have inspired your children this year?

Which friends are you most grateful for?

What lessons do the children learn as you discuss and honor your friendships?

Prayer: Lord, I pray for my children. Clothe them with compassion, kindness, humility, gentleness, and patience. Give them the gift of discernment when it comes to setting boundaries and observing fruit. Give them the joy of fun in their friendships.

DAY 28

Networking

‒‒‒‒‒‒‒‒‒‒‒‒‒‒‒‒‒‒‒‒‒‒‒‒‒ꙮ‒‒‒‒‒‒‒‒‒‒‒‒‒‒‒‒‒‒‒‒

We tend to remember the child who drew us a picture. We remember the youth player who actually listened to the coach at soccer practice. While many teens develop glossophobia (fear of public speaking) around their peers, some maintain courage. We often remember those kids who shined with the light of Christ. Our goal as parents is to develop their leadership skills.

A common reinforcement error parents make is saying, "Oh, that's just his personality." Likewise, we overemphasize personality or temperament when in actuality, it is God burning bright in your son or daughter. Prayer illuminates the Glory of God in your children. We also know that God wants to use our children beyond what we can see. We learn in Matthew 25 that the servant who hid his talent in the ground wasted what his master had given him.

We want to encourage our children to network with other people so their talent will multiply as their sphere of influence grows. Networking tips include being a good listener, remembering names, asking for advice, thinking about long-term relationships, collecting business cards (i.e., kids can write down names), following up, and sending thank you notes.

"Let us pursue the things which make for peace and the things by which one may edify another" (Romans 14:19).

"However you wish to be treated by others is how you should treat everyone else" (Luke 6:31, The Passion Translation).

"Many entreat the favor of the nobility, and every man is a friend to one who gives gifts" (Proverbs 19:6).

Questions:

How can you encourage your children toward being a good listener, remembering names, asking for advice, and thinking about long-term relationships?

If you live far away from friends and family, some keep a family blog; some send paper copies of photographs while others include kids on sending letters, cards or packages. One of the best spiritual networking practices is prayer. In what ways does your family stay in contact and pray for long-distance relatives?

How do you communicate with your kids the power of their Godly influence in others' lives?

Prayer: Lord, I pray for the influence my children can have in business, ministry, and with their families. May their hearts be about giving rather than getting. Bless their networking in the name of Jesus.

DAY 29

Sexual Purity

----------᠗᠍᠍ᠺᠣᠷ----------

So many lives have been ruined as a result of the lies of the sexual revolution. One of the causes of ruin is the widespread use of pornography. As families of Christ, we must rise and declare sexual purity over our families and confront pornography, knocking at the doors of our house.

What are the keys to freedom as we keep the doors closed? First, we must acknowledge that any of us could fall prey to sexual sin, be it pornography, sexting, reading sex ads, adultery, or fornication. Second, you must recognize that pornography is your family's enemy. Parents must have a security plan with technology. Porn is not an option, and you must train your kids, especially your boys, to consider yourself dead to sin and alive to God through Jesus Christ (Romans 6:11-12). Third, fill yourself and your kids with things that are true, pure, excellent and what is admirable (Philippians 4:8). Parents, especially Dad, fill your heart and mind and your kids' hearts and minds with scripture, with worship, Godly beliefs, and by renewing your mind, you will not be conformed to the pattern of this world (Romans 12:2). Give your kids scriptures to memorize and remember – as Dads – we are memorizing and preaching to ourselves.

This war is only won when we acknowledge Jesus. It is an absolute war, especially over our boys. Radical love is the only answer. Parents need to pray around the house for sexual purity. There really is victory, freedom and wholeness in Jesus, and through his beauty and essence, his love can help us shine brightly in this dark world.

Questions:

How does your family wage war against the sexual revolution? How do you reject the lie that porn is a "harmless form of entertainment for sophisticated people?" Instead, how do you train your children to protect their eyes and ears, so they are living victoriously?

What technology do you have in place to protect your children from a sex-obsessed culture? Have you decided on where, when, and what tech may be used, how much time children may be on tech, a family contract regarding tech, and encouraging personal responsibility regarding tech?

How does your family declare purity as one of your highest values?

Prayer: Lord, I pray for sexual purity in my children's lives. I pray for the holiness of heart and mind. I pray for God's protection in every way—around friends' smartphones, watching Superbowl commercials, watching movies, and reading books. I pray for a spirit of protection in Jesus's name!

DAY 30

Relationship with Jesus

―――――――――ᔣᕤᕤᖆ―――――――――

Everything in this devotional is about Jesus. Today, we are joining a Jesus revolution that is a necessity in the face of the culture's moral and spiritual decline. As the world gets darker, we can get brighter. We can shine with more light. Now is the time for us to draw close to the Lord. Take some time to embrace these scriptures and meditate on God's love for you in Christ Jesus.

"Jesus said to him, 'I am the way, the truth, and the life. No one comes to the Father except through Me" (John 14:6).

"But as many as received Him, to them He gave the right to become children of God, to those who believe in His name" (John 1:12).

"For by grace you have been saved through faith, and that not of yourselves; it is the gift of God, not of works, lest anyone should boast" (Ephesians 2:8-9).

Questions:

How can you take the time to worship Jesus as Mary did with her perfume and hair?

How can you worship the Lord with a deeper passion like Zacchaeus, who ran ahead and climbed a sycamore tree along Jesus's path?

When he heard it was the Lord, Peter jumped in the water and swam 100 yards to see Jesus in his bathrobe. How can you remove distractions, jump in, and seek the Lord in prayer right now?

Prayer: Lord, I pray for a deep walk with you, Lord. Out of my love for you and the overflow of my relationship with you, Jesus, I pray that this love will penetrate the deep places of my children's hearts!

DAY 31

Praying Blessings Over Your Child

A bedtime ritual, a consistent sleep schedule, and praying blessings are the keys to a healthy sleep cycle. Establishing a bedtime ritual is the key to establishing a foundation for young children. As kids grow, they learn to brush and floss when the step becomes a habit. Good sleep depends on (1) Turning off Wi-Fi, (2) not using phones/tablets one hour before bed, (3) and getting enough sleep with consistent bedtimes (see previous recommendations).

Praying blessings over your child changes everything in their spirit. Prayer avails much. Prayer brings peace. Prayers are the best blankets. Praying blessings are the best bedtime ritual. Consider praying these blessings over your child every night.

Lord, please bless _____ with:
1. Ability

2. Abundance

3. Angels to go with him/her wherever he/she goes.

4. Assurance of God's love and grace

5. Clear direction for his/her future

6. A controlled and disciplined life

7. Courage

8. Creativity

9. Spiritual perception of God's truths with wisdom and understanding

10. Faith

11. God's favor and man's favor knowing that _____ belongs to the Lord.

12. Good health all the days of his/her life.

13. Bless _____ with his/her future spouse Lord.

14. Hands to bless others with the healing power of God.

15. Gratitude with the past and happiness in the present. Completely fill with the Joy of the Lord.

16. Hope and optimism about the future.

17. A listening ear – to listen well to family and friends, and to the voice of the Lord.

18. Longevity

19. An obedient heart and spirit

20. Peace

21. Pleasant speech and personality

22. Promotion

23. Protection

24. Provision

25. Safety

26. Strength

27. Success

28. Trust

29. Wisdom

30. Goodness and mercy to follow them all the days of their life.

31. The gift of prophecy

32. A radical love for Revival to renew and restore this nation.

33. A personal relationship with Jesus Christ – a deep and intimate love for Jesus.

34. To be an eternal thinker – concerned about the things of God and passionate about the gifts of the Lord.

35. Bless _____ with the fire and purpose to do the will of God and to do all things with great love.

> This is an action step. On this day, take time to pray for God's Grace to make time for you to bless. Ask God to give you the patience to slow things down from the rush. Lord, bless me with the patience to lead this family toward stillness and calmness.

Prayer: Lord, I pray that these blessings over my children do not become a legalistic thing. Rather, I pray that my hands and my mouth speak prophesy over my children out of the rivers of true life. I freely bless out of immense faith in my Lord Jesus Christ!

DAY 32

Sowing and Reaping

ꙮ

A lot of families go through difficult seasons where one parent is planting bitterness seeds. Instead of sowing peace, bitterness is being planted. This consists of seeds of unforgiveness, anger, resentment, envy, and bitterness. Bitterness is like a hardy plant that withstands cold winter temperatures. Bitterness leads to criticism, gossip, murmuring, and complaining and eventually reaps a harvest throughout the family and can endure through the seasons. If this is you, allow the Lord to free you and heal you from this deception.

Father, I repent for my involvement in planting bitterness seeds in my family. I ask you to set me free from my self-deception. Let your truth of joyfulness replace my bitterness. Free me from the power that this bitterness has had over my life and over my identity. Free me from falling victim to my past emotional patterns. Lord, set me free from bitterness, anger, criticism, murmuring, complaining, negativity, and joylessness. I renounce all oppressive forces that promote bitterness in my life.

We need to teach our children the powerful lesson of sowing and reaping, which is a law of life. "Your grumpiness can result in back and forth pushing with your sibling." "Negative words reap a harvest of bickering." Rather, fondness and generosity reap bonding and joyfulness.

"Do not be deceived, God is not mocked; for whatever a man sows, that he will also reap" (Galatians 6:7).

"Sow for yourselves righteousness; reap in mercy; break up your fallow ground, for it is time to seek the Lord, till he comes and rains righteousness on you" (Hosea 10:12).

Questions:

How can you educate your children on what we reap will be sown? What we give out, we get back. When we are unkind, cranky, or mean, or harsh, it plants seeds for the future.

How can you teach your children to pay attention to the seeds they sow? Love is a seed. So is money. Studying, preparation, planning, reading, and practicing all influence what we reap?

What are you deciding to plant in your children? How about your own life? Are you quick to blame, or are you examining your heart and asking the Lord to show you what you have planted in your own life?

Prayer: Lord, I pray for the freedom to sow your goodness and the fruits of the Holy Spirit into my family's lives. May our family sow and bear good fruit for the Glory of God!

DAY 33

Hurt & Pain

Life is full of injuries and pains. Kids are active. They run, jump, climb, try to break records, and fall, resulting in tons of injuries. Of course, there are minor bumps and bruises like cuts and scrapes. There's the growing pains and moans. There's the injuries like bruises that you soothe with an ice pack wrapped in a wet cloth to bring down the swelling. Then there are the strains and sprains of torn muscles and tendons that are experienced in the midst of baseball, basketball, soccer, and gymnastics. Then there are fractures – broken bones in the midst of getting tackled or falling off a skateboard—what a joy to know that children recover from these hurts and pains.

Here is a stereotype that captures many differences with parents: "Well, I think you should be climbing trees," the father replies, "but your Mom would not like that." Regardless of your parental level of risk-taking, building emotional muscle and resilience is scriptural. Injuries can be early opportunities to teach kids how to use hard times to grow in Christ and learn to share testimonies. One of the best ways to help our kids get ready for real life is to reflect on how God wants to use hurts and pains. This will prepare them for the more serious hardships of life.

"Have I not commanded you? Be strong and of good courage; do not be afraid, nor be dismayed, for the Lord your God is with you wherever you go" (Joshua 1:9).

"My brethren, count it all joy when you fall into various trials, knowing that the testing of your faith produces patience. But let patience have its perfect work, that you may be perfect and complete, lacking nothing" (James 1:2-4).

Questions:

How can I speak about "God's purpose" in the midst of hurt and pain my children are going through?

How can I convey empathy and compassion to my children while teaching them to be fearless and unafraid?

A.W. Tozer once stated, "What comes to mind when we think about God is the most important thing about us." What kinds of thoughts do you want to emerge in your children when they are experiencing pain and hurt?

Prayer: Lord, I pray for safety for our children. I also pray for family resilience to bounce back after trials. Help us to stay resilient as we keep our focus on Jesus Christ.

DAY 34

The Word of God

The word of God breathes life. Families can develop different strategies on incorporating bible memorization. Let today be the day to strategize. Talk to God and ask him how you can incorporate a memorization plan for your family. Utilizing different kinds of memory consolidation such as visual memory (index card), auditory memory (saying the verses out loud), rehearsals (repeating out loud), and other strategies (i.e., singing, whispering, voice memos/audio recordings, writing). Some families have a Monday verse, and they memorize a new verse every week. Other families reward kids for memorizations by Friday.

Verses for kids

Jesus Christ is the same yesterday, today and forever (Hebrews 13:8).

Let everything that has breath praise the Lord (Psalm 150:6).

Trust in the Lord with all your heart (Proverbs 3:5).

I am with you always (Matthew 28:20).

Your word is a lamp to my feet and a light for my path (Psalm 119:105).

Every word of God proves true (Proverbs 30:5).

Whatever you do, do everything for the glory of God (1 Corinthians 10:31)

The Lord gives wisdom (Proverbs 2:6).

Trust in the Lord forever, for the Lord God is an everlasting rock (Isaiah 26:4).

Be kind to one another (Ephesians 4:32).

Questions:

Some families have a verse at dinner. What is your word of God strategy?

What scripture verse speaks to your family life right now?

In what ways does your family pray together? Jesus not only taught his disciples how to pray, he encouraged them to pray together (Matthew 18:20).

Prayer: Lord, I pray for the right strategy for our family. Help me to take the time to patiently help our children find the verse in their bible. Give me the wisdom to discuss real-life examples of how the verse applies to our life during our family discussions.

DAY 35

The Psychology Behind Patience

᧞᧟᧞

Reinforce Gratification Delay as early as possible to facilitate patience and strength in this area. Practically, start children young by practicing marshmallow tests on a regular basis. A four-year-old is given a marshmallow. If he can wait 20 minutes, then he gets an additional marshmallow. If a child does not succeed, parents can train them to learn how to wait for something better. Of course, this is best generalized to other things, and healthier food choices if possible.

Emphasize how much better things are by waiting in discussions and family meetings. It is helpful to let this play out in practical life. We can undercut ourselves – you can have that shirt when you save enough money. But we get that shirt the next time we are at the store when a kid is begging for it. That undercuts our initial plan. Motivated parents are mindful of delaying gratification in multiple ways for their children. Play challenge games that involve waiting & patience. For example, a family goes to Dairy Queen and sits on tables waiting 10 minutes before they order. It is clearly communicated that the "wait time" is not a punishment, but rather, a reminder of learning to delay gratification. Youth can get annoyed but are easily swayed with humor. If parents turn these types of things into games, it turns fun fast! As examples: parents can incorporate spelling games with prizes during wait times; or, on the 4th Saturday of the month, every five minutes of waiting can increase the size of the Blizzard.

"Be completely humble and gentle; be patient, bearing with another in love" (Ephesians 4:2, NIV).

"A wrathful man stirs up strife, but he who is slow to anger allays contention" (Proverbs 15:18).

Questions:

What are your family strategies for reinforcing patience?

In what ways is your family patiently waiting on the Lord? One of the very best discussion topics is waiting for God to answer prayer, reveal a particular answer, or show us his hand over time.

How can your family learn to wait, listen and be quiet? When does your family appreciate nature, remain screen-free, and talk about placing a high premium on patience?

Prayer: Lord, I pray for gift of patience. I pray for gratification delay as we persevere with patience. May we be joyful in hope, patient in affliction, faithful in prayer.

DAY 36

Raising Secure Character

———————— ୭୧୨୧ ————————

One of the things that parents need to be aware of and pray about is the pressure that girls experience regarding beauty and attractiveness standards. For 60+ years, beauty standards have been imposed upon girls since the Barbie doll hit the market in 1959. The decades old controversy seems to pale compared to the effects of growing up in a sexual anarchy in the present. Nowadays, we have kids exposed to the use of "photoshopping" to falsify looks. Slimming waists, airbrushing, modifying muscles and smoothing skin are done to achieve a so-called perfection. Girls report that the pressure to look good is the worst part of being female.

Images of the idealized body have permeated every aspect of popular culture. Due to a long history of advertising media distorting perceptions of beauty, girls have to fight against the perception that their primary power is how they look. The Kingdom of God is different than worldly values. In the Kingdom of God, character and who you are is more important than personality, physical beauty, and sexual power.

"She opens her mouth with wisdom, and on her tongue is the law of kindness" (Proverbs 31:26).

"Blessed is she who believed, for there will be a fulfillment of those things which were told her from the Lord" (Luke 1:45).

"I will praise you, for I am fearfully and wonderfully made" (Psalm 139:14).

"Charm is deceitful and beauty is passing, but a woman who fears the Lord, she shall be praised" (Proverbs 31:30).

Questions:

As you shape your children, a key question to return to regularly is: Is your motivation internal or external?

How do you convey that character and Godly identity is more important than personality, physical traits, and beauty?

What events in your family past have influenced who you are today? What decisions (by you or others) have cost you greatly? How have you rebounded from the pain of those mistakes? What is God doing now to bring you closer to the man or woman of God and the best parent you can be?

Prayer: Lord, I pray for freedom from the culture's influences and beauty pressures for my children. Build children's character & the fear of the Lord. I declare freedom and strength for our girls and our boys.

DAY 37

Valuing Failure

Have you ever taken the time to reflect on your failures? This isn't a dreaded over-emphasis on the past. This isn't a "dig the skeletons out of the closet" type of exercise. Rather, this is a refreshing exercise that builds optimism for parents. However, it takes some work; it may feel both pleasant and unpleasant and requires times to reflect deeply. What are those setbacks that made you stronger?

The purpose of this failure reflective exercise is to identify those lessons learned, failures experienced, and key significant moments. Taking time to feel and walk down the failure path reminds us that God brought good out of pain, healing out of hurt, and increased faith on our journey with the Lord.

Our children are going to go through some difficult times: rejection by friends, physical injuries, significant emotional setbacks, loss and failures. Perspective from our failures helps us to see how the Lord carries us and sustains us with the Grace that we need.

"For a righteous man may fall seven times and rise again, but the wicked shall fall by calamity" (Proverbs 24:16).

"For God has not given us a spirit of fear, but of power and of love and of a sound mind." (2 Timothy 1:7).

"Do not rejoice over me, my enemy; when I fall, I will arise; when I sit in darkness, the Lord will be a light to me" (Micah 7:8).

Questions:

What failure in your life have you remained bitter about? How can you give this failure (no matter how big it seems) over to our very Big God who works all things together for his good?

What can you teach your children today about God's love and immense goodness despite our shortcomings and failures?

What are your biggest failures in life? Life is hard, but God is good. How can you teach your children to move forward, live powerfully and fearlessly, and embrace the Lord's plan for their lives?

Prayer: Lord, I pray for my children. Even now for future crosses that they will carry. Strengthen resolve. Bless them with grit. Draw them close to you, in Jesus's name!

DAY 38

Divorced (Single) Parenting

Divorce is extremely painful. Parents going through divorce feel immense pain due to the loss of love and unmet emotional needs, the reality of a destroyed dream, and the felt heartbreak from the break up of the family. During the first few months of a divorce, parents go through severe phases of grief. During these emotional ups and downs, the children act as a great distraction from the pain and a reminder of the parents' actions or decisions leading to the end of the family dream.

Judicial circuit parenting plans often include children's rights that include having the right to have two parents to love without fear of anger or guilt from the other parent; and to develop an independent and meaningful relationship with each parent. Taking this to the next level, parents have an opportunity to teach their children about honor when they speak about their children's other parent.   Speaking with honor about your ex-spouse teaches a valuable lesson to children. Speaking good into your children's relationship with their other parent is a Godly action.

Every single person reading this has been affected by divorce—either you are divorced, you grew up in a divorced family, or someone very close to you has been or is going through a divorce. One of my favorite quotes is from the Christian movie Breakthrough: "Yesterday is not ours to recover, but tomorrow is ours to win or lose." This is especially true for children. No matter what has happened, love for children is key as children go from one home to two homes.

"This is my comfort in my affliction, for your word has given me life" (Psalm 119:50).

"For I know the plans I have for you,' declares the Lord, 'plans to prosper you and not to harm you, plans to give you hope and a future'" (Jeremiah 29:11, NIV).

Questions:

How can this quote fit into your family life experience: "Yesterday is not ours to recover, but tomorrow is ours to win or lose?"

How can you release the past and move into the future with what God has for you. Mark Twain once said, "Sail away from the safe harbor. Catch the trade winds in your sails. Explore, Dream. Discover." How does this fit with what God has for you?

Do you (or any family members) maintain grudges or bitterness from the past? What and who do you need to forgive to experience the fullness of freedom that Jesus Christ has for you?

Prayer: Lord, I pray for my children or other's children as they cope with divorce. I pray for a selfless focus on making this day bright for the kids.

DAY 39

Divorced (Single) Parenting

───────── ෙ෬෬ ─────────

I grew up in a divorced home. It was painful. A divorce produces excruciating pain over time. One of the long-term effects of divorce is growing up with two homes and two sets of realities. In some situations, this is a necessity and a relief. In many situations, children now have two distinct subjective realities that are not intertwined. Some children can grow up with two homes, and there is nothing integrated about the two homes. Adequate communication between parents helps alleviate the pressures. Bringing toys, sharing experiences, ex-spouses being great friends and talking through issues, and active inquiries enhance the integration of these realities.

Taking it to the next level, active prayer time at each home brings healing. In addition to speaking with honor about the ex-spouse, actively engaging in prayer time for "Mommy" ("Mom") or for "Daddy" ("Dad") at "our other home" is vital for the Spirit of the family and for the healing of the family.

Divorced parents are trained to keep "adult stuff" from the kids for several reasons. Today's entry is about your healing. Follow these steps as you ask God to heal your memory. If you are not divorced, make today's devotional about intercession—pray for a family member or friend whose children are negatively impacted by divorce.

- I ask you, Holy Spirit, reveal a memory related to my divorce you want to heal.
- I choose to express my frustration, hurt, and pain to you, Lord.
- Lord Jesus, I invite you into this memory.
- [Quiet yourself, listen, allow him time. Receive his healing].
- Thank you, Lord, for healing my painful memory.

Questions:

What image represents my healing? (If applicable) Ask your son or daughter to describe the image that represents their healing. You may walk them through some feelings. Invite God's love into those feelings.

How am I handling this divorced relationship? Am I honoring my ex, the children's mother or father? Am I speaking prayer and spirit-filled and faith-filled words into these relationships?

How can I enhance the integration of my children's two subjective realities through building a bridge of connection?

Prayer: Lord, I receive my healing with confidence. I receive the gift of time to allow you to work. I accept you as the way maker, one who is always working even if I don't feel it.

DAY 40

Forgiveness

————— ୬୨୧ —————

Father in Heaven, I forgive anyone who has negatively criticized my parenting. I confess the sin of believing lies that are distorting my Godly identity as a parent and causing me to see myself as less than who I am as a parent in Christ. I renounce and break agreement with the lie that I am a defensive parent, a reactive parent, an overly stressed parent, or a defective parent. I receive God's truth that says I am warm, patient, gentle, merciful, nurturing, and loving.

Every one of us is prone to letting negative residuals into our thought process. These residuals can be bitterness, resentments, unforgiveness, or judgments. A lot of what's underneath our anger is blaming and assumptions. The answer to freedom is forgiving ourselves and forgiving those who we blame or who we maintain assumptions about.

I forgive my parents for ways they let me down or lacked love. I forgive myself for any of my shortcomings, mistakes, or failures. I affirm that I have a God-given identity as a parent. I choose to make God the final authority on all of my decisions as a parent.

Matthew 6:9-13

Our Father in heaven,
Hallowed be Your name.
Your kingdom come.
Your will be done
On earth as it is in heaven.
Give us this day our daily bread.
And forgive us our debts,
As we forgive our debtors.
And do not lead us into temptation,
But deliver us from the evil one.
For Yours is the kingdom and the power and the glory
forever. Amen.

Questions:

Is there anyone I need to forgive for any negativity and unlove?

How can I convey to my children the fullness of freedom that comes with letting go of all resentments and bitterness?

Dear Jesus, I ask for forgiveness. I receive your grace and forgiveness. Give me the humility to convey to my children how I am imperfect – with shortcomings, mistakes, and sins. However, give me the wisdom to point the direction to our Heavenly Father, who is perfect in all ways.

Prayer: Lord, I release any agreements I made with resentments and bitterness in my heart. I renounce and release agreements with negativity in the name of Jesus. I release and forgive my parents for any failures or lack of love. I release and forgive my co-parent for any failures or lack of love. I ask you, Lord, to instill within me total forgiveness. I realize and forgive any specific individuals who have criticized my parenting. I pray wholeheartedly for each of my children. I pray that my children will come to know the power and the freedom that comes with forgiveness. I pray that the blessing and freedom that comes with a life of forgiveness will reign in the thoughts and hearts of my children. I pray for profound and immense forgiveness! Bless my children in the powerful name of Jesus Christ of Nazareth!

About Author

---∂⟨∂⟨---

Daniel J. van Ingen, Psy.D. is a licensed clinical psychologist, a sports psychologist, and has been dubbed the Sarasota Parenting Doctor for his work with families. Featured on ABC-7, and a national speaker in over 120 cities and 30 states over the last 10 years, he is co-founder and president of Parenting Doctors. He is the author of *Anxiety Disorders Made Simple: Treatment Approaches to Overcome Fear and Build Resiliency.* His latest book, *You Are Your Child's Best Psychologist: 7 Keys to Excellence in Parenting,* is loaded with the latest and best information from the research and 100's of interviews with parents and professionals.

Go to www.parentingdoctors.com for a great resource on all things parenting. Get a free ebook and subscribe to our regular Parenting Doctors newsletter for the latest and best information on parenting that will inspire, encourage, educate, and motivate you with the best mission on earth. For more information on Dr. van Ingen's psychology practice, go to www.danvaningen.com

Dr. van Ingen also helps manage the Facebook Page Christian Recovery Resource, one of the largest pages in social media. Founded in 2012, this page aims to inspire, heal, and encourage people with the love of Jesus Christ as we all recover from sin and are saved by grace. Visit our Facebook page @ChristianRecoveryResource

Made in the USA
Monee, IL
20 January 2021

58183766R00095